Philadelphia, 1756

by Ann Takman
illustrated by Joanne Friar

HOUGHTON MIFFLIN BOSTON

Printed in China

ISBN-13: 978-0-547-02998-6
ISBN-10: 0-547-02998-5

9 10 11 0940 15 14 13
4500443494

In the 1700s, many people sailed to America from other countries. Many of them were poor. They hoped to find work in America's growing cities. Many of these people went to the remarkable city of Philadelphia.

There was lots to do in Philadelphia!
If you just got off the boat,
you might go to the market.
That's where all the crowds were.
Some people were there to sell food.
Others were there to shop.

You might be amazed by the amounts of fruit and meat for sale! You could buy some bread at a bakery and eat it as you looked around the city.

You might walk past Pennsylvania Hospital. It was the first hospital built in America. Benjamin Franklin helped start it! Franklin was a man of many accomplishments, as you will see.

You might also see the State House. Workers finished building it in 1756. Twenty years later, something very important would happen here!

In 1776, Americans wrote a famous document in the State House.
It said Americans could not be ruled by any other country.
This document said Americans were free!

Back in the 1700s, you might also go into the State House to see the Library Company.
It was the first public library in America.
Ben Franklin helped start it, too!

Ben Franklin was a busy man
in a busy city.
The lightning rod was one of
his many inventions.
He designed one for his home.
As a result, lightning didn't hurt
the house!

You might also see people reading
Poor Richard's Almanack.
Ben Franklin composed
and printed it.
You might hope to achieve
as much as Franklin did!

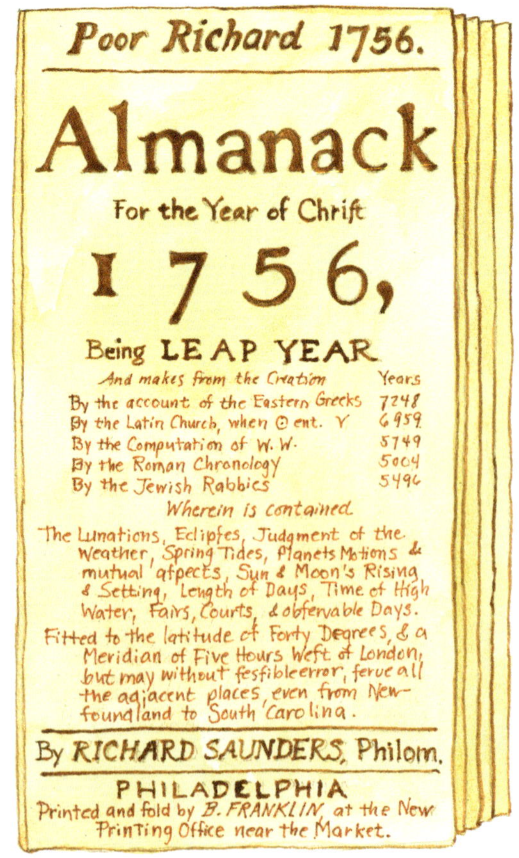

Poor Richard 1756.

Almanack

For the Year of Chrift

1756,

Being LEAP YEAR

And makes from the Creation	Years
By the account of the Eastern Greeks	7248
By the Latin Church, when ☉ ent. ♈	6959
By the Computation of W. W.	5749
By the Roman Chronology	5004
By the Jewish Rabbies	5496

Wherein is contained

The Lunations, Eclipfes, Judgment of the Weather, Spring Tides, Planets Motions & mutual afpects, Sun & Moon's Rising & Setting, Length of Days, Time of High Water, Fairs, Courts, & obfervable Days.

Fitted to the latitude of Forty Degrees, & a Meridian of Five Hours Weft of London, but may without fesfible error, ferve all the adjacent places, even from New-foundland to South Carolina.

By *RICHARD SAUNDERS*, Philom.

PHILADELPHIA

Printed and fold by *B. FRANKLIN*, at the New Printing Office near the Market.

Responding

TARGET VOCABULARY **Word Builder** Make a chart listing some of Benjamin Franklin's accomplishments. Copy the chart below and add more accomplishments. Write why each was important.

Accomplishments	Why Important
invented the lightning rod ? ?	lightning didn't hurt house ? ?

Write About It

Text to World Write a few sentences that explain why Benjamin Franklin's accomplishments were important. Use the Word Builder to help you.

accomplishments	**designed**
achieve	**inventions**
amounts	**remarkable**
composed	**result**

TARGET STRATEGY **Visualize** Picture what is happening as you read.

Word Teaser Which vocabulary word rhymes with *believe*?